Best of Friends 2

The yearbook of Creative Monochrome

C000117239

Editor

Roger Maile ARPS

*CREATIVE
MONOCHROME*

BEST OF FRIENDS 2
The yearbook of Creative Monochrome
Editor: ROGER MAILE ARPS

Published in the UK by Creative Monochrome Ltd
20 St Peters Road, Croydon, Surrey, CR0 1HD.

British Library Cataloguing-in-Publication Data:
A catalogue record for this book is available
from the British Library

ISBN 1 873319 20 7
First edition, 1995

ISSN 1359-446X

Printed in England by The Bath Press,
Lower Bristol Road, Bath, Avon.

Introduction

Roger Maile

I was fortunate enough in the early days of Creative Monochrome – in the middle of a severe recession – to realise that a small specialist publisher would need Friends to see it survive. Friends of Creative Monochrome was formed in November 1992 on little more than a whim and a prayer that there were sufficient monochrome enthusiasts around the world who would care enough to sustain the venture I had embarked upon. Less than three years later, with well over 4,000 Friends in nearly 50 countries, there is a little more substance to the dream.

It was in a similar spirit of relatively unfounded optimism that I launched the idea of a yearbook of members' work at the end of 1993. Given that a year earlier we had not managed to raise enough images for a proposed calendar, this enthusiasm may have bordered on the foolhardy rather than the brave. In the event, the entries flooded in and demonstrated my intuitive belief that a wealth of photographic talent was waiting to be 'discovered' and revealed to an unsuspecting world. Despite the foreboding of the doom merchants, both the quantity and quality of the submissions showed that monochrome photography was alive and well.

So it was that the first edition of *Best of Friends* emerged in October 1994. The excellent entry enabled the production of a stimulating and inspirational book, which was received with enthusiasm by that most telling of critics, the marketplace. One of the most pleasing aspects of this reception was the number of people who became Friends as a result of having seen the book. Additionally, nearly 200 Friends took the trouble to vote for the BoF Awards (see page 5), many commenting on how difficult they had found the task of narrowing down their selection.

At the time of inviting entries for this present volume, it was too early to know the commercial fate of the first edition, so the project remained largely an act of faith. Yet again, the Friends – old and new – rallied to the cause, producing a splendid entry of 3,196 images representing the work of 338 Friends. From this huge entry, 148 images by a total of 101 Friends have been selected and are presented in this edition.

I described in some detail the motivation behind Creative Monochrome and, for want of a better description, its philosophical thrust, in the first issue of *Best of Friends*, so I will not repeat it here. Suffice it to say that the purpose of Creative Monochrome is to foster the appreciation and enjoyment of quality monochrome photography – of all styles and subject matter – and to provide the opportunity for excellent work to be shared with the widest possible audience. This is achieved not just through the publication of books, cards and posters, but by acting as a catalyst for other activities, such as postal portfolios, workshops and seminars.

I will, however, write a little about the process of submission and selection, to provide the reader with some idea of how the images shown here came to be chosen from such a large and high quality entry.

The conditions of entry were kept as simple as possible, without limits on the quantity, style or subject matter for submissions. Neither were there any limits on entrants in terms of amateur or professional status. Membership of Friends of Creative Monochrome was a requirement, but as this costs nothing and involves no purchase commitment, it was hardly an impediment.

It was made clear from the outset that the selection would be my own choice. I will forgive those who regard this as a simple symptom of meglomania, as indeed it may be, but I have never felt that a committee was the best forum for decision-making. Whoever it was who said that a camel is a horse designed by a committee has my vote. Inevitably, the single selector will be more vulnerable to the accusation of personal favouritism or bias in terms of style and subject matter, but I still feel selection should be on the basis of conviction rather than compromise.

The selection process took place throughout the six months during which entries were invited. The first round selection took place as soon as each entry was received, choosing which prints had a chance of inclusion and erring on the side of caution – if in doubt, keep it. At the end of each month, the second round involved pooling the prints received during the previous four weeks, so that the relative merits of entries could be considered in the context of the overall standard of entry. Needless to say, the third round, representing the final selection for the book, took place during May after all the entries had been received.

This may seem an unduly elaborate process, but it has the merit of testing the 'staying power' of the prints. I feel it is important that images in a book can sustain interest: you want the reader to be able to return to the prints both to enjoy established favourites, and possibly to discover hidden depths in such images, but also to find new pleasures in those which perhaps had less immediate impact. This is probably the main difference between the selection processes for a book and a salon-type exhibition. In the latter, hidden depths may remain concealed because the prints fail to catch the selectors' eyes in the few seconds during which the yes/no decision is made. In selecting for the book, I have the luxury of a 'maybe' and the time to reflect and review.

The luxury of reflection is no more evident than during the final selection round, which takes place over several days. By this stage, factors such as the flow of images through the book and the need to achieve some degree of balance between subjects and styles come into play. Luck can play a part in this – for example, I knew from the moment I first saw it that I wanted to include Jerry Keogh's powerful and moving study, *Auschwitz*. But I was equally aware of how unlikely it was that I would find an image that could live with it on an adjacent page. The option of showing the image on its own was not at all attractive because it would have meant starting or ending the book on this haunting note. When Rick Cook's *Implements of Warfare* came out of the envelope, I knew immediately that the two images would not just work together, but actually draw strength from each other. I don't know what the chances are of two such images being submitted entirely independently in the same year, but I know that I said a quiet 'thank you' to the Great Photographer in the Sky.

Such 'coincidences' were surprisingly common. It may sound rather weird, but during this final stage, it often seemed that the book was shaping itself. To my mind and eye, so many of the images on page-spreads were just made for each other, and all I had to do was to be alert enough to recognise them.

There were, however, many images which I liked very much but which did not get selected. In most cases this was because of the need to avoid any particular subject area becoming unduly dominant: particularly popular areas included landscape, water and tree studies. At the other extreme, some subject areas (such as sport) were so under-represented that I felt it was not possible to cover the area adequately and that it was better to omit the subject than have it stand out like a sore thumb.

Another of the pressures on my mind during the final selection was to avoid the book being too much like its predecessor in terms of content. The last thing I want is for *Best of Friends* to become stale and predictable. But given the success of the first issue, I was equally anxious not to throw the baby out with the exhausted developer. You will be the judge!

It has been my pleasure and privilege to make this selection and I admit to being proud to be able to share these images with you. I hope that they will bring you as much enjoyment and stimulation as they have for me. And I also hope that you will reflect this by making your own selection for this year's BoF Awards.

Six medals – one gold, two silver, and three bronze – are awarded each year

Voting for the BoF awards

Gold medal, 1994-95
Belvedere I
John Nasey

Silver medal, 1994-95
Earth and sky
Michael Maguire

Silver medal, 1994-95
Northumberland waterfall
Peter Dixon

The images in *Best of Friends 2* are the equivalent of an exhibition of Friends' work. As is customary in such exhibitions, there are awards for a small number of prints which especially capture the judges' attention. All Friends of Creative Monochrome are invited to be the judges and to cast votes to determine the award winners.

Here's what to do. Each Friend has a maximum of 10 votes to award. Within that limit, you may allocate the votes as you see fit. For example, you can choose 10 prints to give one vote each; or you could give all 10 votes to one image; or somewhere in between. Votes can only be used in whole numbers. Friends may not vote for their own work.

To vote, for each image selected, write down the image number (*not* the page number), photographer and number of votes awarded. Please also include your own name and address (or membership number). Send your vote to: Creative Monochrome Ltd, 20 St Peters Road, Croydon, Surrey, CR0 1HD, England, **to arrive by 31 March 1996**, or vote by fax on 0181-681 0662.

To join the Friends of Creative Monochrome, or for further information, write to the above address or telephone 0181-686 3282.

The prints on this page are the six medal winners in the first BoF Awards (and, of course, are not eligible this time).

Bronze medals, 1994-95

above: Alpine storm
David Oldfield

opposite above: Hedge & fence, Edale
Hugh Milsom

opposite below: The gate
Tom Richardson

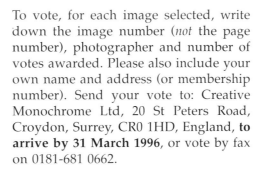

Index of contributors

(The index references are to image numbers, rather than page numbers)

Portfolio

1
Eype, Dorset
Joy White

2
Grasses and ice on rock
Len Perkis

3
Dead leaves and ice on branch
Len Perkis

4
Divided flow
Peter Clark

5
Eroded dome
Rob Gray

6
Weir
Gordon Western

7
Going, going!
Hazel Sanderson

8
Simply reeds
John Devenport

9
Cloudy puddle
Chris Wilkes

10
Winter in Holland
Ton van der Laan

11
Alpine outlook
David Oldfield

12
Single tree, Yorkshire Wolds
John Reed

13
Lone tree
Michael Milton

14
Ambergate, Derbyshire, 1991
Andrew Tymon

15
Birch wood, West Wickham
Nick Duncan

16
Sussex woodland
Bill Wisden

17
Scrub oak
Michael Milton

18 **Tree line**, *John Nasey*

19 **Elemental**, *Michael Kersting*

20 **Pine tree, West Blean Wood**, *Trevor Crone*

21 **Grassland**, *Clive Vincent*

22
Memories
Kathleen Harcom

23
The nude
Brian Ebbage

24
Nude at the gazebo #2
Roy Elwood

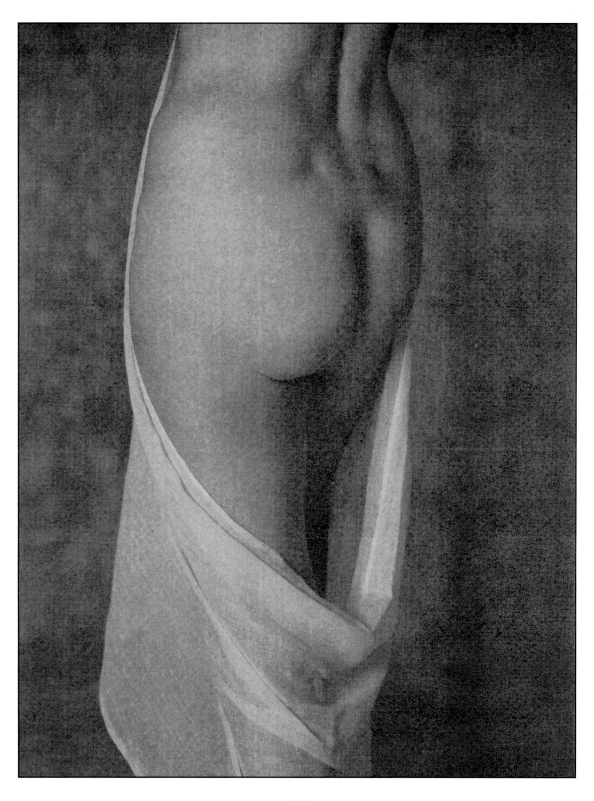

25
Figure study #2
Mike Salter

26
Untitled
Ray Spence

27
Bathed in light
David Miller

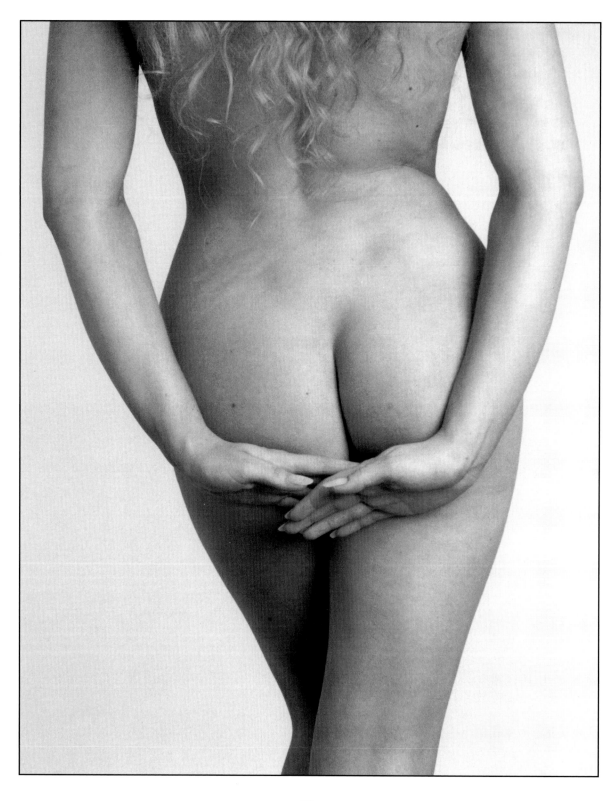

28
Xquisite
Denis Morley

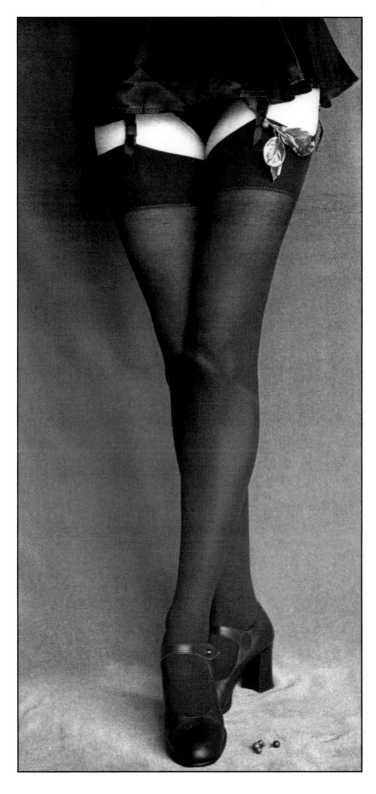

29
Black stockings
Linda Sutton

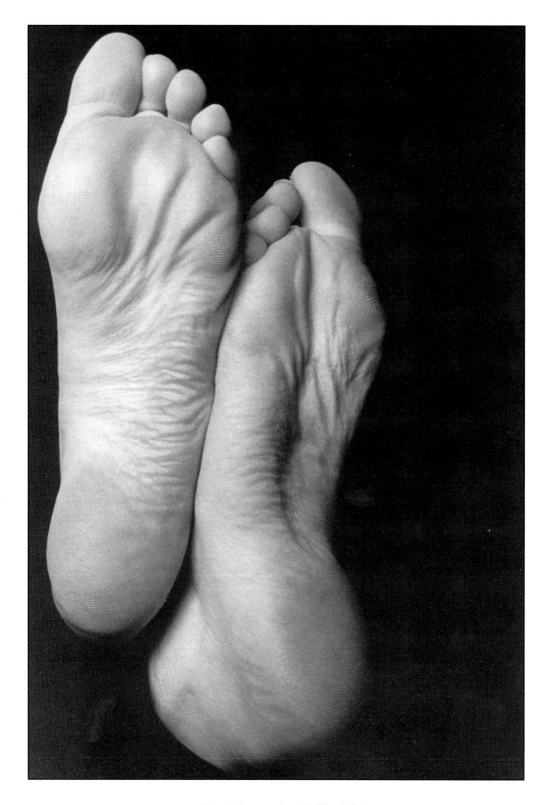

(above) 30 **Sole to sole**, *Phillip Atkinson*
(opposite top) 31 **The hand**, *Charles Baynon*
(opposite below) 32 **Legs**, *Charles Baynon*

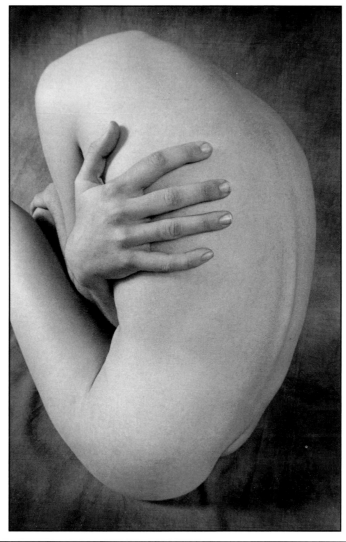

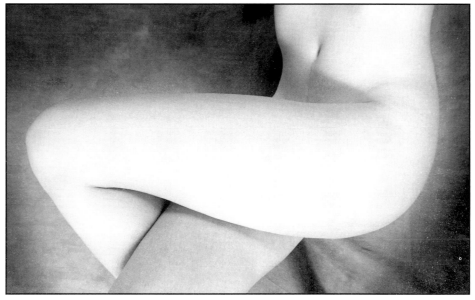

33
The leaf
John Devenport

34
Tree folds and textures
Hugh Milsom

35
Canyon shapes
Rob Gray

36
Antelope Canyon II
Alfons Endl

37
Divided
Stephen Smith

38
Grasses and leaves
Tim West

39
Inca wall, Cuzco, Peru
Jenifer Roberts

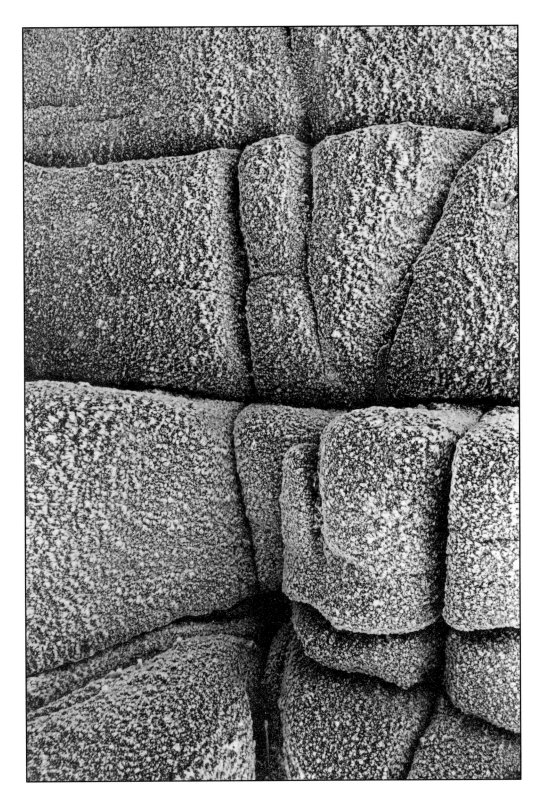

40
Untitled
Jiri Bartos

41
Ice fragment design
John Devenport

42
Ice coins
Hazel Sanderson

43 **Ice pattern**, *Arnold Hubbard*

44 **The seashore**, *Marianne Shipp*

45   **Ice I, Little Crowden Brook**, *Paul Murphy*

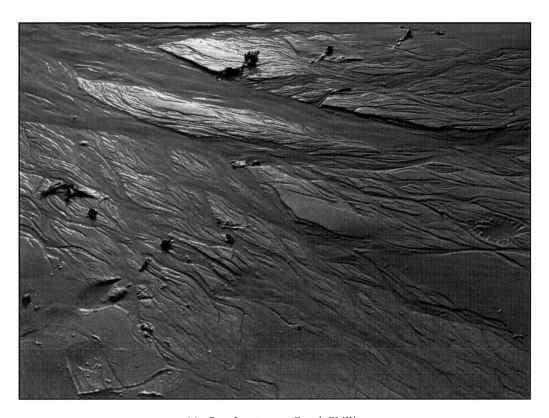

46   **Sand pattern**, *Frank Phillips*

47
Sand pattern
Paul Damen

48
Black sand
Neil Souch

49
Weathered groyne
Michael Milton

50
Storm damage, Camber
David Dixon

51
Hopeless
Zoltán Molnár

52
Woman, resting
Klaus Peters

53
Man and bicycles
Alan Millward

54 **Mary and Sally Army doorway**, *Alan Millward*

55 **Solitary**, *Andy Wilson*

56
Gospel singers, Weymouth beach
Frederick Everett

57
Untitled
Brian Walker

58
Alan with his gypsy caravan, Devon
Joy White

59
Mr and Mrs J Skinner
John Philpott

60
Up front, Malawi
Anne Newell

61
Three boys
Geoff Davies

62
Home and garden
Bill Carden

63
The house on Walland Marsh
David Dixon

64
Chateau de Brésis
Anne Newell

65
Mont St Michel
Trevor Buttery

66
Warkworth Castle
Albert Snell

67
Windmills, La Mancha
John Nasey

68
Lily pond
Kathleen Harcom

69
Poppy field
Albert Snell

70 **One fine day**, *David Dixon*

71 **Glen Clachaig, Mull, Scotland**, *Tom Richardson*

72 **Trees II**, *John Nasey*

73 **Rannoch Moor #1**, *Peter Clark*

74
Mountain winter
Tom Dodd

75
Glencoe
John Nasey

76
The Road
Alan Fowler

77
Dutch 'mountains'
Ton van der Laan

78 **Mountain cairn, Brim fell, Cumbria**, *Tom Richardson*

79 **Aiguile du Dru**, *Tom Dodd*

80
Cumbrian winter
Baron Woods

81
Coeden Ar Y Llech
Margaret Salisbury

82
Reincarnation
Trevor Crone

83
Have faith
Priscilla Thomas

84
Hayton Parish Church
Peter Rees

85 **In the old priory**, *Peter Rees*

86 **Gawsworth Church, Cheshire**, *W N Teale*

87
Estate cottage
Reg Ireland

88 **Ornate ceiling**, *Mike Hale*

89 **Underground parking à l'Italienne, Lyon, France**, *Françoise Sauze*

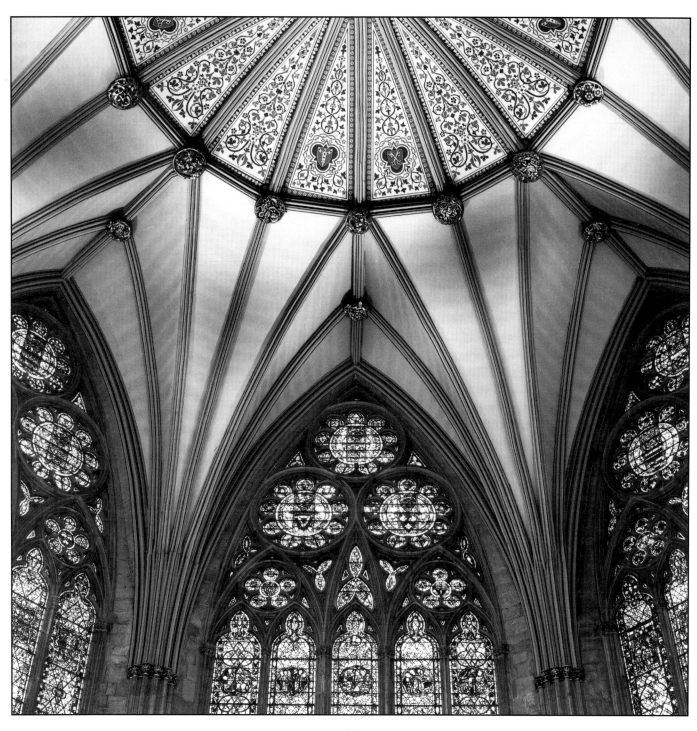

90
Chapter house, York Minster
Mark Snowdon

91
Time
David Betts

92
Mother and daughter, 4th July
Anne Crabbe

93
Spooky cottage
Mike Coles

94
Lusia
Peter Rees

95
Headbound – a self portrait
Neil Gibson

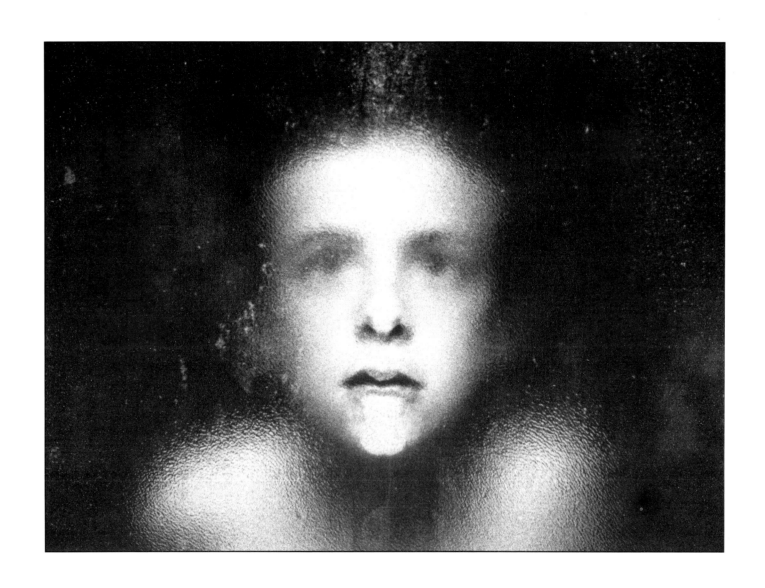

96
Nightmare
Roger Scott

97
Hot house dreamer
Angela Ford

98
Broken dreams #3 – the lost souls
Trevor Crone

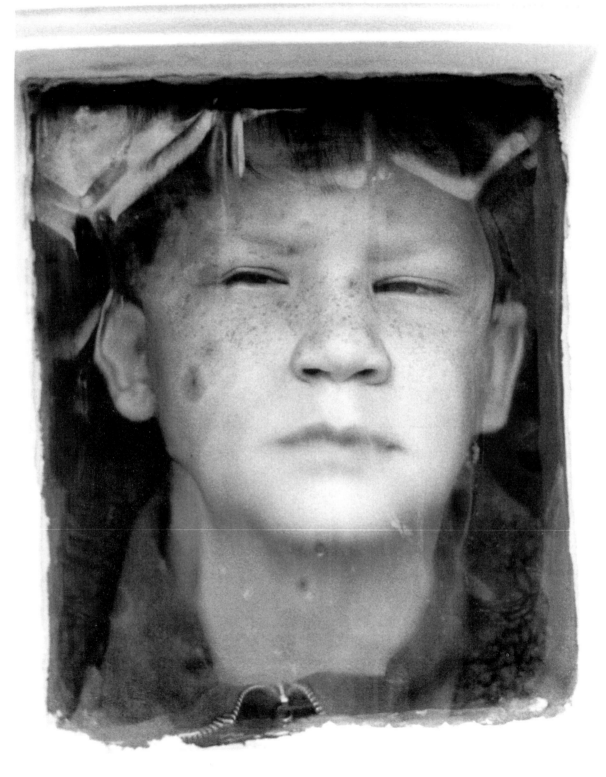

99
Boy at window
Michael Kersting

100
Sisters
Colin Johnston

101
Belonging III
Sue Davies

102
Yorkshire lad
Bill Carden

103
The sisters
Charles Baynon

104
Style of the renaissance
John Worton

105
Lucy 11
Roger Noons

106
Rachel
Sue Keeling

107
Nicaise, African dancer
Roger Maile

108
Michael #1
David Miller

109
Carnevale
David Wraith

110
Rats tails
Christine Chambers

111
Cabinet of dreams #1
Paul Warner

112
Cabinet of dreams #3
Paul Warner

113
Leaves and fruit
Rod Wheelans

114
Daisies
Joan Rooker

115
Garlic
Arnold Hubbard

116
Pear and chopper
Den Reader

117
Garden seat
Reg Ireland

118
Early morning on the bench
Hazel Sanderson

119
Amid decay #3
Patricia Jones

120
From a bygone era
Peter Dixon

121
Auschwitz
Jerry Keogh

122
Implements of warfare
Rick Cook

123 **Beech leaves**, *Ray Spence*

124 **Water ballet**, *Clive Haynes*

125
Frond
Clive Haynes

126
Funnel
Peter Maschkan

127
Untitled
Jiri Bartos

128
Broken column, Ephesus
Jack Whittle

129
Slebech
Mark Richards

130
Wildwood
Clive Haynes

131
The pony
Patrick Reilly

132
The eye
Mike Heller

133 **Sheep with shepherd**, *Bill Carden*

134
Windswept
Tom Richardson

135
Taken in the rain
Ron Eaton

136
Beach bums
Denis Morley

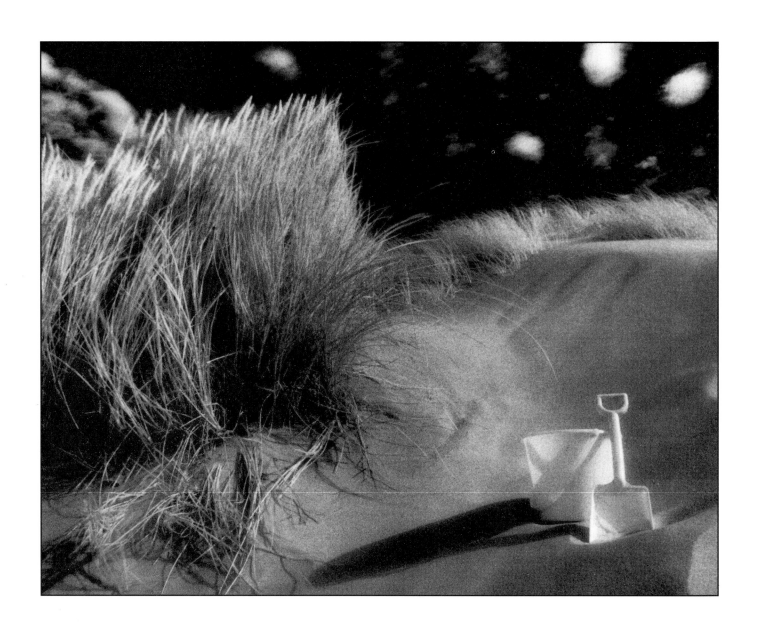

137
All but the sea
Ray Pitt

138
Martha and boat, Devon, 1988
Roy Holley

139 **Life line**, *Jim Ford*

140 **Newborough light**, *Peter Clark*

141 **On Beachy Head**, *Nick Duncan*

142 **Seven Sisters**, *Brian Ebbage*

143 **Kennack Sands, Cornwall**, *Trevor Crone*

144 **Sand path**, *Frank Phillips*

145 **Connemara seascape**, *Mark Snowdon*

146 **Spey Bay**, *Tom Brydon*

147
Malvern winter
Allan Wood

148
On yer bike!
Vince Rooker

Contributor profiles

Those submitting work for this book were invited to supply a personal photographic profile. Available space has meant that these have had to be edited to a brief outline – with apologies for any vital information omitted or inaccuracies introduced! In a few cases, profiles were not provided and it proved impossible to get information prior to the print deadline. The italicised numbers in brackets at the end of each entry are the reference numbers of the images in the portfolio (ie not the page numbers). There is a glossary of abbreviations used in the profiles on page 144.

Phillip Atkinson *(Buckinghamshire)*
Having learned monochrome printing at evening classes, Phillip joined a camera club and has never looked back. Many of his photographs are taken in and around Milton Keynes to try to dispel the 'concrete jungle' legend. *(30)*

Jiri Bartos *(Czech Republic)*
(40, 127)

Charles Baynon *(Shropshire)*
A professional photographer for 11 years, Charles has been commissioned by a number of blue chip companies and has had pictures published in national newspapers. He has had a number of exhibitions of his private work, covering landscape, still life and, more recently, the nude. *(31, 32, 103)*

David Betts *(Isle of Wight)*
In his youth, David first drifted into (and out of) photography as a second string to his rock music ambitions. More recently, he has discovered a real passion for the medium, making images which combine mystery, eroticism and fantasy. His first book, *Island Maidens*, was published by Creative Monochrome in 1995. *(91)*

Tom Brydon *(Avon)*
As a commercial, industrial and architectural photographer, Tom spends his free time combining his love of the British countryside with pictorial photography. He finds the freedom of not having to work to clients' instructions more challenging (and more difficult) than working to a brief. *(146)*

Trevor Buttery *(Staffordshire)*
A keen amateur and a member of Newcastle (Staffs) CC, Trevor is particularly interested in monochrome landscape work, usually using grainy or infrared films. He has recently begun to dabble with computer image manipulation. *(65)*

Bill Carden *(Middlesex)*
A member of High Wycombe CC and the London Salon, Bill gained his RPS Fellowship in 1971 and has served on the RPS Pictorial and Licentiateship distinctions panels. He is currently a member of the RPS distinctions moderating board. He is best known for his candid photography of people. *(62, 102, 133)*

Christine Chambers *(Surrey)*
Having joined Selsdon CC in the mid-1980s, Christine felt encouraged by the members and her husband to try monochrome printing. She gained her ARPS in 1994 with a panel of toned monochrome prints. Her photography is currently following her interest in graphic design and in exploring various toning techniques. *(110)*

Peter J Clark *(Staffordshire)*
A member of Cannock PS for over 15 years, Peter is a well known judge and lecturer. He achieved his RPS Fellowship for his monochrome landscape work. With over 700 exhibition acceptances, including over 100 awards and 6 FIAP/PSA gold medals, Peter is a holder of the AFIAP distinction. *(4, 73, 140)*

Mike Coles *(Avon)*
Having worked with colour slides for five years, Mike has been exploring monochrome printing for only one year as a medium for expressing pre-visualised images. His preferred subjects include sport, people, still life and landscape photography. *(51)*

Rick Cook *(Derbyshire)*
Rick's photographic work is a response to places and objects that he encounters in everyday life and when travelling. Much of his monochrome work reflects his fascination for the landscape, although his family also features prominently in his photography. *(122)*

Anne Crabbe *(Buckinghamshire)*
(92)

Trevor Crone *(London)*
Having become interested in photography in 1973, Trevor has progressed to have work published in magazines and books, and as postcards and greetings cards. He has exhibited

widely and has won several national photographic competitions. He is the competition secretary for Greenwich PS. (20, 82, 98, 143)

Paul Damen (Norfolk)
Paul, who holds a degree in photographic media studies, is an Associate of the British Institute of Professional Photography and the RPS and a member of UPP. He is well known as a judge and as a tutor on photography. He has made two videos on landscape techniques. (47)

Geoff Davies (Lancashire)
Having started taking a serious interest in photography while on national service in Cyprus, Geoff set up a home darkroom when demobbed. A long-time member of Bolton CC, his main interest has been in candid and reportage photography, but Geoff says that "as he grows older" he has a stronger feeling for the landscape. (61)

Sue Davies (Buckinghamshire)
Sue became hooked on photography as a result of enrolling on a City & Guilds modular photography course. Encouraged to visit galleries and exhibitions, she was particularly impressed by John Blakemore's Inscape exhibition and freely admits the obvious influence on her own work. She is an Associate of the RPS. (101)

John Devenport (London)
John has been making monochrome images for about 15 years and is an active member of Beckenham PS and the Mirage Group. He gained his ARPS in 1988 with a panel of pictorial landscapes. His approach to photography involves a keen sense of observation, attention to detail and an appreciation of strong design elements. (8, 33, 41)

David Dixon (Kent)
A Fellow of the RPS, David enjoys club life at Tonbridge CC and submits work regularly to the international exhibition circuit, gaining the gold medal for best monochrome print at the British Open in 1995. Most of his work recently has been with infrared film, which he uses to create a sense of drama and austere mood. (50, 63, 70)

Peter Dixon (Tyne & Wear)
Peter has been interested in photography for over 30 years, is a member of Tyneside CC and Whickham CC, and lectures widely on monochrome photography. With five other North East photographers, Peter formed the Imprint Group, whose aim is to promote photography through exhibitions around the North East. (120)

Tom Dodd (Gwynedd)
Tom's photographic interest spans some 24 years and is inseparable from his involvement with the outdoor environment. A well known lecturer, exhibitor and judge, Tom gained his FRPS in 1979. He is a member of the London Salon and the licentiateship panel of the RPS. His first book, *Cwm Orthin*, is about to be published in the CM Contemporary Portfolio series. (74, 79)

Nick Duncan (Kent)
Nick works almost exclusively in monochrome and describes his work as mainly pictorial/landscape. He has had some work published and has recently been experimenting with infrared film. A member of Bromley CC, he gained his Licentiateship and Associateship of the RPS in 1990 and 1994 respectively. (15, 141)

Ron Eaton (Devon)
Ron has had a serious interest in photography for around 12 years, gaining his ARPS in 1984. For the past 10 years, he has been secretary of the Plymstock Co-Op CC. Preferring monochrome for any subject, he describes himself as "roaming Dartmoor in desperate search for pictures". (135)

Brian Ebbage (Norfolk)
An enthusiastic club photographer for 15 years, Brian gained his Fellowship of the RPS in 1991 for a portfolio of monochrome landscapes. Enjoying the unreality of black and white, Brian's subject interests include landscapes, infrared photography and the nude – sometimes all in the same print. (23, 142)

Roy Elwood (Tyne & Wear)
Much of Roy's life centres around photography, especially monochrome – an enduring first love. Recently, he has shifted away from individual images towards sets of prints on themes, such as water, nudes and dancers. He gained his Fellowship of the RPS in 1994 with a panel of nudes, each featuring parts of the male and female body. (24)

Alfons Endl (Germany)
Alfons has been a photographer for over 50 years, preferring monochrome, and has been a member of a camera club since 1956. He uses mainly 35mm equipment, favouring Kodak's Technical Pan film processed in his own brew. He has had many acceptances in national and international competitions. (36)

Fred Everett (Essex)
Although he also has an interest in landscape and portraiture, Fred describes his favourite subject matter currently as "life as it passes by". He enjoys the challenge of trying to create some form of order or composition from what passes in front of his eyes. He is a member and ex-President of Loughton CC. (56)

Angela Ford (Kent)
Angela enjoys all kinds of subjects, from people to landscapes, and works mainly in monochrome. She has recently become very interested in exploring the creative possibilities of infrared film. A member of Bromley CC, Angela gained her Licentiateship and Associateship of the RPS in 1987 and 1989 respectively. (97)

Jim Ford (Bedfordshire)
Although interested in photography for several years, Jim has taken a serious interest since joining Bedford CC in November 1993. He has gained many competition successes and has recently achieved acceptances in the East Anglian

Federation annual exhibition. He is now working towards RPS distinctions. *(139)*

Alan Fowler *(Tyne & Wear)*
Alan is a member of Gateshead CC and gained his Associateship of the RPS in 1989. He describes his main interest in photography as "capturing light, mood and feeling within the print. The subject matter is not that important – it is the combination of these ingredients, in my opinion, which makes the image successful". *(76)*

Neil Gibson *(Cleveland)*
Having gained A-level photography through evening classes, Neil is a now a member of the Gallery Photo Group in Middlesbrough, Stokesby PS and a monthly printers' club, the Castle Group. His most recent work focusses on the effects of nature and time on man-made objects. *(95)*

Rob Gray *(Australia)*
Rob specialises in monochrome landscapes using a 5x4 camera. A keen bushwalker, he often spends days alone in the wilderness. Rob's images are his way of bringing some of the peace he finds in the Australian bush back to town and sharing it with others. He is a regular exhibitor and is represented by several galleries. *(5, 35)*

Mike Hale *(Clwyd)*
(88)

Kathleen Harcom *(Hampshire)*
Although enjoying many aspects of photography, Kathleen's main interest is landscape work. She has successfully completed a number of college courses in photography and gained her Associateship of the RPS with a panel of monochrome infrared images. *(22, 68)*

Clive Haynes *(Worcestershire)*
Clive has been making pictures for some 30 years. His subjects are, mostly, natural things. He particularly enjoys the creative opportunities of multi-exposure and the subtle use of hand-tinting. He is a longstanding member of Worcestershire CC and a founder member of Infinity Plus fine print group. *(124, 125, 130)*

Mike Heller *(Gwynedd)*
Mike has been involved in still photography for 25 years, with particular interest in monochrome work. This has resulted in publication in many newspapers, magazines and books. He has also had work exhibited locally in North Wales, where he is an active member of Caernarfon CC. *(132)*

Roy Holley *(Northamptonshire)*
An artist by training, most of Roy's images revolve around family life and his daughters' activities, such as riding and sailing. He describes his photos as "a bit like snapshots" as he likes to retain the immediacy of photography. Although none of his shots are posed, he works hard at composition, never cropping his negatives. *(138)*

Arnold Hubbard *(Tyne & Wear)*
Arnold has been a member of Sunderland PA for almost 25 years. His work has been seen in many national and international exhibitions. A Fellow of the RPS and holder of the EFIAP distinction, Arnold is a popular lecturer and regular judge on the club circuit. *(43, 115)*

Reg Ireland *(Northamptonshire)*
Although discovering a love for monochrome photography in 1947, working life and family commitments meant that it was not until retirement in 1985 that Reg was able to fully indulge his photographic interest. Since then he has gained Licentiateship and Associateship of the RPS and is now seeking inspiration for an FRPS panel. *(87, 117)*

Colin Johnston *(Tyne & Wear)*
Colin has been taking photographs with enthusiasm for more than 10 years, but it was only after joining a local camera club six years ago that he caught the monochrome bug. He finds working in black and white a source of endless pleasure but also, at times, an enormous frustration – "I am not yet in control!". *(100)*

Patricia Jones *(Kent)*
An active member of Sevenoaks CC and UPP, Patricia has been taking photographs for over 10 years, gaining her ARPS in 1991. She enjoys capturing the ever changing, and often dramatic, light in the landscape and also seeking out and isolating small close-up details formed by nature within the landscape. *(119)*

Sue Keeling *(West Midlands)*
Sue has been a keen club photographer since 1983 with Wall Heath CC and Smethwick PS. She has had work exhibited in local, national and international exhibitions, receiving awards at all levels. She was one of the first recipients of the PAGB awards for photographic merit at the distinction level. *(106)*

Jerry Keogh *(Denmark)*
Jerry's submitted profile was a model of brevity, wit and modesty: "1988: started photography; 1995: still trying!" *(121)*

Michael Kersting *(Surrey)*
Five years ago, Michael attended evening classes in monochrome photography, but a house move postponed the application of his newly acquired skills until 1994, when he joined Carshalton CC. He describes himself as at the bottom of the learning curve, but hoping to progress through practice and experimentation. *(19, 99)*

Ton van der Laan *(Netherlands)*
Ton became interested in monochrome photography about 20 years ago and progressed through membership of a local camera club. He started by concentrating on architecture, but has subsequently become more and more interested in nature photography. *(10, 77)*

Roger Maile *(Surrey)*
Roger is the director of Creative Monochrome and consequently has depressingly little time to pursue his own

photographic interests – mainly people photography and a growing fascination with digital imaging. He is an Associate of the RPS, a member of Selsdon CC and often judges and lectures on the local camera club circuit. *(107)*

Peter Maschkan *(London)*
(126)

Dave Miller *(Tyne & Wear)*
Although he started taking photographs 20 years ago, it is only in the last six years that Dave has taken it more seriously. He enjoys producing prints to be hung on his wall or to be exhibited to a wider audience. Recently he has moved away from single images towards developing small sets of photographs on a theme. *(27, 108)*

Alan Millward *(West Midlands)*
Alan specialises in monochrome images of people, for which he was awarded the Fellowship of the RPS in both Applied and Pictorial categories. He is a past President of Solihull PS, past chairman of the Midland Salon, a member of the London Salon and a member of the RPS Licentiateship panel. *(53, 54)*

Hugh Milsom *(Hertfordshire)*
Best known for his landscape photography, Hugh has been making photographs for over 30 years. Reflecting his many successes in national and international exhibitions, he has gained the MFIAP distinction. A member of Ware PS and Shillington CC, Hugh's first book, *Earthsong*, has just been published by Creative Monochrome. *(34)*

Michael Milton *(Devon)*
Michael took up photography in 1977. In the mid-80s he moved to London and worked for four years as a photographer's assistant, before starting his own business. After taking an HND in photography at Swansea, his direction changed towards natural items, landscape and man-made objects within a landscape. *(13, 17, 49)*

Zoltán Molnár *(Romania)*
(51)

Denis Morley *(Nottinghamshire)*
Working almost exclusively in monochrome, Denis's favourite film is Kodak Infrared. He has gained acceptances in both national and international exhibitions. He is a founder member of the Triangle Group of creative photographers who share a commitment to the monochrome image as fine art. *(28, 136)*

Paul Murphy *(Manchester)*
Paul's main photographic interests are natural formations (particularly rocks and ice) in the nearby Peak District, and buildings in the inner city region of Manchester. He tries to record the character of these subjects in the manner of portraits, showing them in the best possible light. *(45)*

John Nasey *(Channel Islands)*
Although only taking up photography some 10 years ago,

John has already progressed to Fellowship of the RPS and has been entering national and international exhibitions since 1988. Since 1989, he has been teaching monochrome photography courses at the Jersey Art Centre. He was the gold medal winner for the first edition of *Best of Friends*. *(18, 67, 72, 75)*

Anne Newell *(Cornwall)*
Anne took up photography some 25 years ago, but after a prolonged period of abstinence from the hobby, took it up again a few years ago with renewed vigour. One fruit of this enthusiasm was the gaining in 1993 of her Licentiateship of the RPS. A member of a small, but friendly and enthusiastic, camera club, Anne's main interest is in landscape photography. *(60, 64)*

Roger Noons *(West Midlands)*
A member of Smethwick PS and a regular exhibitor in national and international exhibitions, Roger is better known for his colour work. After 28 years in club photography, however, he has decided that he can better express some of his ideas in monochrome, and we can expect to see more from him in this medium. *(105)*

David Oldfield *(Australia)*
David enjoys bushwalking in the Victorian Alps to find monochrome landscapes that encapsulate his feelings about the Australian bush. Currently the senior vice-president of the Australian Photographic Society (APS), David is an Associate of both the RPS and APS. *(11)*

Len Perkis *(Norway)*
Since taking early retirement six years ago, Len has devoted most of his time to making photographs. His main subject interests are landscape, nature and travel. Len has had images published in many prestigious books and magazines and a major shipping line has used many of his landscapes to decorate its ships. *(133, 134)*

Klaus Peters *(Germany)*
Klaus has been taking photographs since 1967 and has seen his work accepted for exhibitions, magazines, books and calendars. His main interest is in monochrome photography and his preferred subjects include travel, landscape and portraits. He has been awarded the Artist distinction in the FIAP awards. *(52)*

Frank Phillips *(Devon)*
A retired chartered surveyor, Frank says he has been "a photographer of only average achievement for over 40 years". His primary interest is in landscape and coastal images. An Associate of the RPS, he describes his current ambition as "getting a print accepted for *Best of Friends*" – so what's next? *(46, 144)*

John Philpott *(Hampshire)*
John was awarded the MBE for his services to the Ordnance Survey, where he was official photographer for 10 years. A Fellow of the RPS, he is a well known lecturer in photographic clubs and his work is widely represented in

national and international exhibitions. He specialises in photographing people and his book, *Face the Camera*, was published by Creative Monochrome in 1994. *(59)*

Ray Pitt *(West Midlands)*
Ray started photography about 11 years ago after buying a Praktica 35mm camera and attending night school "to find out how it worked". He subsequently joined a local camera club, gaining some successes in competitions and exhibitions. After a period of absence, he has recently been encouraged to take up the challenge again. *(137)*

Den Reader *(Norfolk)*
Den has a string of one-man exhibitions to his name and his work has been seen in several publications (including a full portfolio in *Minolta Mirror*). He currently has 15,000 original images lodged with a major picture library, bringing his work to a wide and varied audience. *(116)*

John Reed *(North Yorkshire)*
John has been making monochrome images for about six years and is an active member of the York PS. He holds the Licentiateship of the RPS. *(12)*

Peter Rees *(Shropshire)*
A club photographer, exhibitor and RPS member, Peter gained his Associateship of the RPS in colour slides, but in recent years his main enthusiasm has been monochrome printing. With over 1000 exhibition acceptances to his name, including FIAP medals and other awards, he has earned the EFIAP distinction. *(84, 85, 94)*

Patrick Reilly *(Ireland)*
Patrick has been taking photographs since the 1970s, and enjoys a wide variety of aspects of the hobby, although still finding monochrome the most exciting medium. He writes, "While I think about my work, I don't feel the need to explain it in detail: if other people like it, I see that as a bonus." *(131)*

Mark Richards *(Dyfed)*
Mark became enthralled with photography at the age of 16. During a short spell at college, he decided he preferred practise to theory, resulting in 15 years' work as a commercial photographer. Now he longs to get back to his roots in monochrome landscape, reportage and children's portraiture. *(129)*

Tom Richardson *(Lancashire)*
Tom has been interested in photography for 20 years, with serious intent during the last nine. An Associate of the RPS and holder of the BPE(2 star) distinction, Tom's work has been accepted by a number of salons and national exhibitions. His preferred subject is landscape and his ambition is to publish a book. *(71, 78, 134)*

Jenifer Roberts *(Surrey)*
A Fellow of the RPS, Jenifer exhibits regularly and gives workshops on landscape photography and monochrome printing. She works only in monochrome, placing great emphasis on meticulous printing. A book of her photographs,

Spirit of the Place, was published by Creative Monochrome in 1992, and her second book, *Connections*, will be published in 1996. *(39)*

Joan Rooker *(Northumberland)*
A photographer for 16 years and an Associate of the RPS, Joan lectures and judges in the Northern Counties Photographic Federation, and is a past chairman of Morpeth CC. She is secretary of a UPP circle and currently a member of the UPP executive. *(114)*

Vince Rooker *(Northumberland)*
Vince has been a photographer for over 40 years and is currently chairman of Morpeth CC. He is an associate of the RPS and is active in the Northern Counties Photographic Federation as judge and lecturer. Following redundancy in 1983, he established a successful wedding and portrait business, helped by Joan. *(148)*

Margaret Salisbury *(Clwyd)*
Margaret has a string of photographic distinctions to her name, including two Fellowships of the RPS, the FIAP Excellence award, and Associate membership of the PAGB. She is a member of the London Salon and, as an Ilford sponsored lecturer, Margaret lectures throughout Great Britain. *(81)*

Mike Salter *(Avon)*
Mike has been interested in photography for about 12 years, but over the last four years has become more involved in his own processing and printing. An active member of Bristol PS, he works only in monochrome, making mainly landscape and figure images. Mike gained his LRPS in 1994. (25)

Hazel Sanderson *(West Yorkshire)*
Hazel is best known for her evocative landscape photography as featured in her Creative Monochrome book, *The Dales of Yorkshire*. She describes her photographs as "a simple statement of a sensitive awareness of the beauty of the natural world, combined with a sense of wonder and respect". *(7, 42, 118)*

Françoise Sauze *(London)*
After a degree in video, Françoise turned to still photography, working at first in colour and more recently in monochrome. Her interest is in recording social and environmental issues. She is currently using her still images as the base for digital montages. *(89)*

Roger Scott *(East Sussex)*
An active member of Eastbourne PS for over 25 years, Roger's monochrome work uses strong, but simple, composition and design. Whilst having a strong interest in landscape photography, his more recent work has taken a selective and graphic approach to picture-making. He exhibits his work nationally. (96)

Marianne Shipp *(Northumberland)*
Marianne joined Hexham PS in 1977, working in colour slides and Cibachrome prints and she still presents a joint slide

show, *Badgers, Birds and Bluebells*, with photographer husband Jim. She started monochrome work eight years ago and her main interest is in landscape photography. *(44)*

Stephen Smith *(Derbyshire)*
Stephen has been a professional photographer for over 10 years, but over the last five has diversified into video production. Thus his monochrome image-making is a form of relaxation and a far cry from the 'day job'. He has never before exhibited his work or tried to get it published, preferring to keep his craft as a personal activity. *(37)*

Albert Snell *(Tyne & Wear)*
Albert has been a member of Sunderland PA for over 30 years and is past president of the Northern Counties PF. A lover of the open air, he particularly enjoys recording the various moods of the sea. He finds the camera an incentive to get out in all weathers and a valuable companion on long walks. *(66, 69)*

Mark Snowdon *(North Yorkshire)*
Mark developed his interest in photography in 1986 whilst living in South Africa. He works almost entirely in monochrome, normally using medium format cameras, with a preferred combination of Agfa APX25 film and Rodinal developer. He became an Associate of the RPS in 1991 and is currently working towards the Fellowship. *(90, 145)*

Neil Such *(Devon)*
Neil has been interested in pictorial photography for over 35 years and says that living in Devon ensures his love for landscape photography is never exhausted. He particularly enjoys involvement in postal portfolios, both as a platform for his work and a source of inspiration. A founder member of the CM Western Chapter folio, he is also secretary of two RPS folios. *(48)*

Ray Spence *(Warwickshire)*
Ray's passion for photography was kindled while taking a degree in microbiology and, after a 12 year stint as a biology teacher, he chose to lecture in photography and media studies. He is a Fellow of the Royal Photographic Society and has lectured and exhibited widely in the UK. In 1994, Creative Monochrome published a portfolio of his work, *Form & Fantasy*. *(26, 123)*

Linda Sutton *(Essex)*
Married with two teenage sons, Linda has been a photographer for several years, during which she has taken City & Guilds photography courses. She enjoys hand-colouring photographs, finding that this adds a three-dimensional quality to the images. *(29)*

W N Teale *(Cheshire)*
An active member of Crewe PS, he has been making monochrome images for around 15 years. His main interest is in pictorial work, for which he finds monochrome particularly suitable. His work has been exhibited at several venues in the UK. *(86)*

Priscilla Thomas *(East Sussex)*
Priscilla acquired her first slr in 1991 and discovered photography as a means of creative expression. She gained her LRPS in 1992, ARPS in 1993 and – on her fifth attempt "with blood, sweat and tears" – the Fellowship in 1995. She has enjoyed numerous successes in national and international exhibitions. *(83)*

Andrew Tymon *(Lancashire)*
Having started to take photographs in 1981, Andrew gained a degree in photographic studies at the University of Derby in 1993. His main subject is the landscape, both naturally occurring and imagined. His motivation is to bring back and share the things that he has seen. *(14)*

Clive Vincent *(Cornwall)*
Clive became interested in photography 12 years ago and has specialised in monochrome for the last 7 years, concentrating particularly on landscape studies of the most rugged areas of his native Cornwall. Entirely self-taught, he has had several solo exhibitions, national and international salon acceptances, and a number of images published. He is a member of Penwith Photo Group. *(21)*

Brian C Walker *(Wiltshire)*
Brian is a commercial, industrial and wedding photographer, who has also been teaching photography in Swindon for several years, encouraging a wealth of new talent and organising exhibitions of their work. Brian is an Associate of the RPS and has had his images published in a number of photographic magazines. *(57)*

Paul Warner *(Devon)*
Paul is a photographer and sculptor who is using his work to "explore thresholds within myself and the world as I experience it". He admits that many of his images perplex him: "I find you can explore without knowing what you are going to find". He gained the fellowship of the RPS for a series entitled, *Cabinet of Dreams*. *(111, 112)*

Tim West *(West Sussex)*
Tim's photography is purely for pleasure, covering a wide range of subjects, although with a particular interest in motor racing. He has been a member of Midhurst CC for 18 years and is an active member of the Contemporary group of the RPS, gaining his Associateship in 1989. He gained the BPE two crown award in 1994. *(38)*

Gordon Western *(Buckinghamshire)*
Gordon still remembers vividly his wonder and delight as a child at seeing his father's contact prints emerge in the developer dish. It was only 12 years ago that Gordon had the space to create his own darkroom and to "set out on a voyage of discovery which was sometimes enjoyable, but often infuriating and frustrating". *(6)*

Rod Wheelans *(Dumfries)*
Rod has been serious about photography since discovering monochrome some 15 years ago. He acknowledges a debt to club photography which he is repaying by serving on several

committees. He has also started a group, Teamworks, which has exhibited widely in Scotland. Rod holds the Excellence award of FIAP, the PAGB Distinction and is an ARPS. *(113)*

Joy White *(Somerset)*
Joy is a freelance illustrative photographer in her twenties who specialises in landscape, portraiture and documentary work. An Associate of the RPS, Joy's photographs are published regularly and have been shown in various exhibitions. *(1, 58)*

Jack Whittle *(Manchester)*
Jack has taken a more serious interest in photography since his retirement. He particularly enjoys depicting the relationship between the effects of passing time and encroaching vegetation on archaeological sites (preferably ones with minimal interference by restorers). An active club member, Jack is also a Fellow of the RPS. *(128)*

Chris Wilkes *(Wiltshire)*
Although he has been taking photographs since the age of seven, Chris's work became serious about eight years ago after joining a local camera club. His main subject interest is landscape, most of which is of North Wales, where he has held a small exhibition. An Associate of the RPS, his aim is to produce a book of his work. *(9)*

Andy Wilson *(Nottinghamshire)*
Andy is a Friend of, and exhibitor in, the London Salon of Photography, and has acceptances in many national and international exhibitions. He is a founder member of the Triangle group of fine art monochrome printer/photographers and has had his images published in several photographic magazines. *(55)*

Bill Wisden *(East Sussex)*
Bill is a well known lecturer to photographic societies, spending much of his time encouraging others that "all is possible". A Fellow of the RPS, Associate of the PAGB, and a member of the London Salon, Bill is the chairman of the RPS Pictorial distinctions panel. *(16)*

Allan Wood *(Worcestershire)*
Allan became seriously interested in photography and monochrome work about 25 years ago, benefitting from many years membership of UPP. He particularly enjoys landscape and monochrome work. He gained his Licentiateship of the RPS in 1991. *(147)*

Baron Woods *(Lancashire)*
Interested in photography since the mid-1960s, Baron began in monochrome, but soon "graduated" to colour printing, gaining his Fellowship of the RPS. Two or three years ago his interest in monochrome landscapes was rekindled and he now finds this a much more satisfactory medium for portraying light, mood and atmosphere. *(80)*

John Worton *(Nottinghamshire)*
John's images are almost all people pictures, usually in the sphere of 'style/portrait' or 'period narratives' – story-telling pictures in a period context. He finds that self-imposed deadlines, such as his annual one-man exhibition, are a necessary incentive to complete such studies. *(104)*

David Wraith *(Shropshire)*
David started taking photographs in 1979, initially as a colour slide worker, but was bitten by the darkroom bug in the early 1980s when he joined Shropshire PS. His enthusiasm intensified on joining the well regarded print workers at Wrekin Arts Photographic Club. His preferred subjects are landscape and people. *(109)*

Glossary of abbreviations used in profiles

BPE British Photographic Exhibitor – 'crown' awards depending on acceptances in recognised national exhibitions

CC Camera Club

FIAP *(translated as)* International Federation of Photographic Art: awards distinctions of Artist, Excellence and Master, based mainly on acceptances in recognised international exhibitions

PAGB Photographic Alliance of Great Britain

PF Photographic Federation

PS Photographic Society

PSA Photographic Society of America

RPS The Royal Photographic Society (UK): awards distinctions at Licentiate (LRPS), Associate (ARPS) and Fellowship (FRPS) levels, by submission of work for assessment by admissions panels

slr Single lens reflex: a type of camera using a prism and mirror to allow the photographer to view the subject through the camera lens

UPP United Photographic Postfolios.